INCREDIBLE
Kid Edibles™

Beth Brigham

 STARBURST PUBLISHERS®

P.O. Box 4123 Lancaster, PA 17604

www.starburstpublishers.com

To schedule author appearances, write:

Author Appearances, Starburst Promotions
P.O. Box 4123, Lancaster, PA 17604

or call (717) 293-0939.
Website: www.starburstpublishers.com

Cover design by David Marty Design
Photography by Stan Sinclair
Food styling by Rebecca Robison
Illustrations by Beth Rupprecht and Melissa Burkhart
Text design and composition by John Reinhardt Book Design

First printing, February 2002
ISBN: 1-892016-45-1
Library of Congress Catalog Number: 2001090044

Printed in United States of America

Dedicated to the memory of my mother,
Helen Knudsen von Dach,
who taught me that the
little things in life matter a lot.

Contents

Introduction

Parents are often called upon to provide snacks for their child's school, sports team, birthday, or other party. Too often because of time constraints or lack of ideas, they resort to the same old bag of chips or box of cookies. As a preschool teacher, I saw many ho hum snacks brought to school, which were promptly dumped in the trash by the children at snack time. When a fun snack was presented, the kids' faces lit up and they eagerly ate it. And what imaginative conversation flowed around these snacks!

Incredible KidEdibles makes food fun. Snacks become exciting and something to talk about. Cupcakes become cats, peanut butter becomes play dough, and toast becomes an art canvas. Which would you rather eat: boring crackers and cheese or three blind mice? The same old apple slices and animal crackers or a circus carousel? Why eat a roll when you can bite the head off a bread snake?

Teachers, grandparents, parents, kids, and anyone young at heart can enjoy this book of my favorite, easy recipes. There is even a chapter of recipes for play doughs, putties, and paint made from edible ingredients. Get ready for artistic, innovative, fun ideas for parties, holidays, and every day in between. Enjoy this book with the children in your life!

CHAPTER 1

Creamy, Crunchy, Crazy Critters

Most children are fascinated with all things creepy, crawly, or slimy. They love anything warm, fuzzy, and cuddly. This chapter is full of recipes to delight. Snakes. Dogs. Worms. Hedgehogs. Spiders. Bees. Bears. Bunnies. After trying these recipes you may find that your child likes bugs after all!

Snake Bakes

Frozen bread dough
  loaf, thawed (1)

1/4 cup flour

Raisins (12)

1/4 cup melted butter

Food coloring

❶ Divide the bread dough into 6 pieces. Sprinkle a small amount of flour on working surface, and roll each piece of dough to form a snake.

❷ Place 2 raisin "eyes" on each snake.

❸ Mix melted butter with several drops of food coloring and paint onto snake. Place snakes on a cookie sheet and bake for 15 minutes at 350°F.

Nice Mice

18-oz. tube refrigerated
sugar cookie dough

M & M® candies (40)

Raisins (20)

Black shoestring licorice
(80 1-inch pieces)

❶ Freeze cookie dough for 30 minutes.

❷ Remove dough from wrapper, and cut into 30 equal slices. Place 20 slices on ungreased cookie sheets approximately 2 inches apart.

❸ Cut remaining 10 slices into fourths for ears. Shape each small piece into a circle, and attach to mouse "heads." Press 2 M & M® candy "eyes," 1 raisin "nose," and 4 licorice "whiskers" onto each mouse face.

❹ Bake at 350°F for 11 minutes or until lightly browned.

Mice Cupcakes

18.25-oz. cake mix, any flavor

16-oz. tub ready-made pink
   frosting or white tinted
   with red food coloring

M & M® candies (48)

Nilla® wafers (48)

Hershey's Kisses® chocolate
   candies (24)

Black shoestring licorice
   (96 1-inch pieces)

❶ Prepare cake mix as directed on package. Pour into muffin tins lined with paper baking cups. Bake as directed. Frost when cool.

❷ For each cupcake, stick on 2 Nilla® wafer cookie "ears," 2 M & M® candy "eyes," 1 Hershey Kiss® "nose," and 4 licorice "whiskers."

Bear Buns

7.5-oz. package of 10 refrigerated biscuits

Raisins (21)

❶ Lay 7 whole biscuits on a cookie sheet. Cut the 3 remaining biscuits into 7 equal pieces each. Roll each small dough piece into a ball. Press 2 pieces onto each whole biscuit for the ears and 1 small piece onto each whole biscuit for the snout.

❷ Press in raisin "eyes" and "nose." Bake for 10 minutes at 400°F.

Butterfly in the Sky

Celery stalk (1)

*1/4 cup cheese spread
or peanut butter*

Large pretzel knots (4)

Chow mein noodles (4)

❶ Cut celery stalk in half. Fill each stalk with cheese or peanut butter.

❷ Press 2 pretzel knots into each stalk for the butterfly wings and 2 chow mein noodles into the front for the antennae.

Ants on a Log

Celery stalk (1)

1/4 cup peanut butter

2 tablespoons raisins

❶ Cut celery stalk in half.

❷ Spread peanut butter on celery.

❸ Arrange raisin "ants" on top of peanut butter log.

Bananapillar

Bananas (2)

Pretzel sticks (28)

1 teaspoon peanut butter

Raisins (4)

❶ Peel bananas.

❷ Poke 6 pretzel sticks in each side of both bananas for legs, and 2 pretzel sticks on top of each head for antennae.

❸ Using peanut butter for adhesive, attach raisin "eyes."

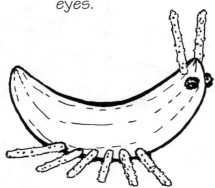

Buzzing Bees

1/2 cup peanut butter

1 tablespoon honey

1/2 cup dry milk

1 teaspoon cinnamon

Sliced almonds (48)

❶ Mix together peanut butter and honey.

❷ Stir in the dry milk. Shape the dough into 24 1/2-inch ovals. Chill for 1 hour.

❸ Dip the flat side of a toothpick into the cinnamon, and press onto the ovals for stripes.

❹ Add almond "wings."

Pear Bunnies

Lettuce leaves (6)

15-oz. can pear halves

Raisins (12)

Sliced almonds (12)

1/2 cup cottage cheese

❶ Lay a lettuce leaf on each plate. Place 1 pear half cut side down on the lettuce.

❷ Press raisin "eyes" and almond "ears" into the narrow end of each pear.

❸ Add a spoonful of cottage cheese for the tail.

Hedgehogs

15-oz. can pear halves

1/2 cup melted chocolate

1/3 cup almond slivers

Raisins (12)

❶ Drain the pears on a paper towel. Dip 3/4 of each pear (wide end first) in chocolate. Place on waxed paper.

❷ While chocolate is warm, stick in almond "quills" and raisin "eyes."

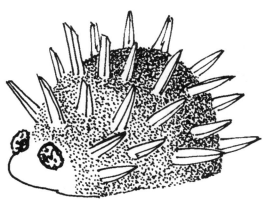

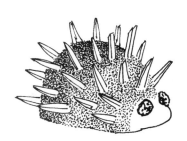

Dirty Worms

16-oz. package Oreo®
cookies

2 cups milk

3.9-oz. chocolate instant
pudding mix

8-oz. tub whipped topping,
thawed

9-oz. clear plastic cups (12)

Gummi worms (24)

❶ Crush the cookies. Set aside.

❷ Combine pudding mix and milk. Mix as directed on package. Chill for 5 minutes.

❸ Stir the whipped topping and half of the crushed cookies into the pudding.

❹ Fill each cup with layers of crushed cookie, pudding mixture, and more crushed cookie mixed with gummi worms. Place in refrigerator for approximately 1 hour.

Flutterbys

Small pretzel knots (48)

7-oz. pkg. caramels

Shoestring licorice
   (48 1-inch pieces)

❶ For each pair of flutterby wings, arrange 2 pretzel knots together, bottom to bottom, on a greased cookie sheet.

❷ Melt the caramels over low heat. Spoon 1 teaspoon of melted caramel over the middle of the wings.

❸ Press 2 licorice pieces into caramel for the antennae.

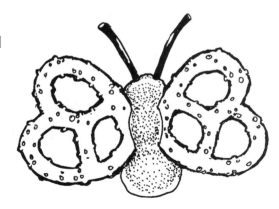

Lady Bugs

1/2 cup white ready-made
   frosting

Red food coloring

Oreo® cookies (12)

1/2 cup raisins

Shoestring licorice (24 1-inch
   pieces)

❶ Mix frosting with several drops of food coloring.

❷ Spread frosting onto right and left sides of tops of cookies, creating ladybug wings.

❸ Add spots to wings with raisins. Press 2 licorice pieces into tops of cookies for the antennae.

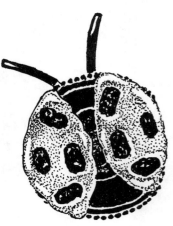

Pear Puppies

15-oz. can pear halves

Dried apricots (12)

Raisins (12)

Grapes (3), cut in half

❶ Place pears cut side down. Place apricot "ears," raisin "eyes" and a grape "nose" on each "puppy."

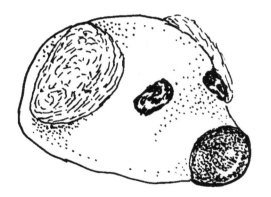

Dalmatian Cupcakes

18.25-oz. cake mix, any flavor

16-oz. tub white frosting

Large marshmallows (12)

Mini marshmallows (12)

Junior Mints® (48)

Small black gumdrops (24)

Black shoestring licorice
   (72 1/2-inch pieces)

1/2 cup mini chocolate chips

Oreo® cookies (24)

❶ Prepare cake mix and bake cupcakes as directed on package. Frost when cool.

❷ Cut all marshmallows in half crosswise.

❸ For each cupcake, place 2 Junior Mints® "eyes," and 1 large marshmallow half "snout." Using frosting as adhesive, attach 1 small marshmallow half onto each mint and place 1 gumdrop "nose" and 3 pieces of licorice "mouth" onto each large marshmallow half.

❹ Using serrated knife, cut Oreo® cookies in half. Stick 1 half in each side of cupcakes for ears. Using frosting as adhesive, place 2 mini chocolate chips on small marshmallows for pupils and the remaining chocolate chips all over the face for the spots.

Dread the Bread Dragon

Long baguette bread loaf (1)

Radishes (3)

❶ Make 10 crosswise cuts in bread, leaving bottom 1/2 inch and one end (approximately 4 inches) uncut. Slice horizontally through 3 inches of the uncut end and force these "jaws" apart.

❷ Peel a small section of 2 radishes to create the whites of the eyes. Attach radish "eyes" with toothpicks. Cut a thin slice from the red skin of the other radish and insert it into the mouth for the tongue. Arrange the body into a curve.

Along Came a Spider

Round crackers (24)

1/4 cup peanut butter

Pretzel sticks (96)

Raisins (24)

❶ Spread 12 crackers with peanut butter. Top with remaining crackers, creating sandwiches.

❷ Stick 4 pretzel "legs" into each side of spider, securing them in the peanut butter.

❸ Add 2 raisin "eyes" in front.

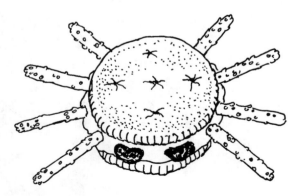

Daddy Longlegs

1/4 cup peanut butter

1/4 cup powdered sugar

1/4 cup chocolate milk powder

Chow mein noodles (32)

❶ Mix together the peanut butter and powdered sugar. Roll 1 tablespoon of this dough into a ball for the spider body and 1 teaspoon of dough into a ball for the spider head. Repeat with the remaining dough.

❷ Place the chocolate milk powder in a bowl, and roll all dough balls in it. Attach heads to bodies by pressing together.

❸ Place 4 chow mein noodles in each side of the spiders for legs.

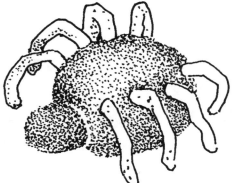

Spider Cupcakes

18.25-oz. cake mix, any flavor

16-oz. whipped topping, thawed

Black licorice twists (192)

M & M® candies (48)

Chocolate decorator sprinkles

❶ Spray muffin tins with cooking spray. Do not use baking cup liners. Prepare cupcakes as directed on package. Cool. Turn cupcakes upside down, and frost with whipped topping.

❷ Insert 4 licorice "legs" into the tops of each side of the cupcakes. Add candy "eyes," and sprinkle with decorator sprinkles.

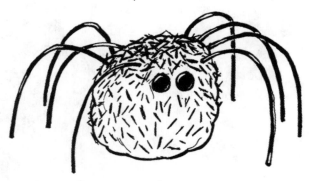

Snails

1 tablespoon cinnamon

3 tablespoons sugar

Sandwich bread (10 slices)

8-oz. tub spreadable cream
cheese

1/2 cup melted butter

Shoestring licorice (60 1-inch
pieces)

❶ Mix together cinnamon and sugar.

❷ Remove crusts from bread. Spread cream
cheese on the bread, and roll up tightly. Cut
each roll into 3 equal pieces.

❸ Dip each piece into the melted butter and
then roll in the cinnamon sugar mixture.
Bake on a cookie sheet
for 10 minutes at
350°F.

❹ Insert 2 pieces of licorice
into the top of each snail for
the antennae.

Tomato Flies

Medium tomatoes (4)

Cucumber, 4 thin round slices

Cherry tomatoes (4)

Tiny dill pickles (4)

Toothpicks (8)

Whole cloves (8)

Mustard (in squeeze
   container)

❶ Make a small slit in each side of medium tomatoes.

❷ Cut cucumber slices in half and insert into slits in sides of tomatoes.

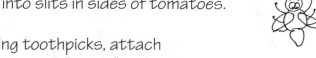

❸ Using toothpicks, attach cherry tomato "heads" to front of medium tomatoes and pickle "tails" to the back of medium tomatoes.

❹ Stick cloves into cherry tomatoes for eyes. Pipe mustard onto the back of the flies for spots.

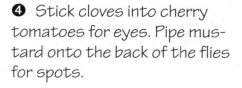

Three Blind Mice

Small rectangular crackers
   (6)

Whole almonds (18)

Sandwich-style cheese
   (2 slices)

Chow mein noodles (18)

❶ Evenly space 3 almonds on each cracker.

❷ Cut each cheese slice into thirds. Cover the crackers and almonds with a slice of the cut cheese.

❸ Insert the chow mein noodles under the cheese at the wide end of the almonds. Microwave or bake in a warm oven just until cheese begins to melt.

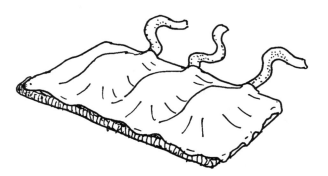

Pecan Turtles

6-oz. pkg. pecan halves (144)

17.5-oz. peanut butter cookie
  dough mix

1/3 cup oil

1 egg

M & M® peanut candies (36)

1/2 cup mini chocolate chips

❶ For each turtle, arrange 4 pecans in a cross shape so ends of pecans are touching on an ungreased cookie sheet.

❷ Stir together cookie dough mix, oil, and egg. Roll cookie dough into 1-inch balls and insert a peanut candy into the center of the ball, closing the dough around it. Place a cookie ball on the middle of each pecan cross. Bake for 11–13 minutes at 375°F.

❸ Remove from oven, and immediately place 2 chocolate chips on top of 1 pecan on each cookie for eyes and several on the back of each cookie for spots.

CHAPTER 2

Boats, Trains, and Airplanes

Get your kids going with these snacks that go. They're sure to sail through the boats, cruise through the trucks and trains, and soar through the airplanes. These snacks are so tempting they'll go fast.

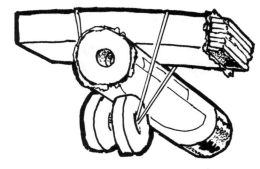

UFOs

15-oz. refrigerated pie crusts

1/2 cup pizza sauce

Thinly sliced ham (4 slices)

1 cup grated cheese, any kind

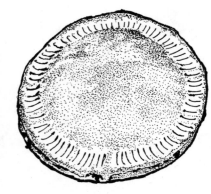

❶ Unfold pie crusts. Using a 3 1/2-inch round cookie cutter, cut out 4 circles from 1 crust. Lay on cookie sheet.

❷ Spread 1 tablespoon of pizza sauce on each. Top each with 1 slice of ham and 2 tablespoons of cheese.

❸ Cut 4 more circles from remaining crust. Place 1 crust on each of the other crusts. Pinch sides together with the tines of a fork.

❹ Bake at 450°F for 9–11 minutes.

Rockets

Bananas (2)

Apple (1)

2 cups popped corn

❶ Cut 2 inches off the bottom of each banana and discard. Cut remaining bananas in half lengthwise.

❷ Lay each piece flat side down on a plate. Core the apple, and cut into 12 equal slices. Lay 2 apple slices near the bottom of each banana with one end touching banana and other end pointing down.

❸ Cut remaining apple slices into small chunks. Place chunks on banana for windows and popped corn at bottom of banana for smoke.

Airplanes

Rubber band

Individual Life Savers® candies (2)

5-piece pack of gum (1)

Life Savers® (1 pack)

❶ Place rubber band through 2 individual Life Savers® candies. Pull ends up and around the ends of pack of gum.

❷ Insert pack of Life Savers® through rubber band on underneath side of gum.

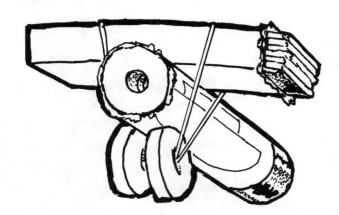

Chew Chew Train

Tacky glue

Life Savers® (1 pack)

5-piece pack of gum (1)

Gold foil-wrapped chocolate
caramel drop (1)

Caramel (1)

Hershey's Kisses® (1)

Round peppermint
candies (4)

❶ Using tacky glue, attach package of Life Savers® onto pack of gum. Be sure to place glue only on the wrappers, not on the candy.

❷ Glue gold-wrapped candy onto one end of Life Saver® roll and caramel onto the top of opposite end of the roll.

❸ Glue Hershey's Kiss® on top of remaining end of the Life Saver roll and 2 peppermints on each side of the gum for wheels.

Cheese Stick Truck

*Individual cheese and
  breadstick snack (1)*

*Mini Reese's® peanut butter
  cups (4)*

Tacky glue

❶ Turn cheese and breadstick package upside down.
Using tacky glue, attach wrapped peanut butter cup
"wheels."

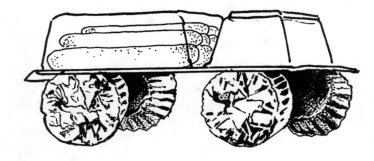

Bananamobiles

MAKES 2

Bananas (2)

Kiwis (2)

Toothpicks (8)

Strawberries (2)

*Blueberries or
   boysenberries (2)*

❶ Peel bananas.

❷ Cut each kiwi into 4 round slices. Attach the kiwi "wheels" to banana "car" with toothpicks.

❸ Using toothpicks, attach strawberry "body" and blueberry "head" for the passengers in the cars.

Cantaloupe Canoes

Cantaloupe (1)

Strawberries (24)

Toothpicks (48)

Blueberries (24)

❶ Cut melon into 8 equal slices, discarding seeds.

❷ Using toothpicks, affix 3 strawberries, equally spaced, into each slice.

❸ Again using toothpicks, affix blueberry "head" onto each strawberry "body."

Tomato/Cucumber Boats

Large tomatoes (4)

Cucumber (1)

Toothpicks (16)

❶ Cut tomatoes into quarters.

❷ Cut round slices from cucumber, and then cut each into halves or quarters.

❸ Attach cucumber "sails" to tomato "boats" with toothpicks.

Lickety Split Banana Boats

MAKES 4

Bananas, unpeeled (4)

2 cups whipped topping, thawed

1/4 cup chopped peanuts

Maraschino cherries (4)

❶ Slit each banana peel on one side, leaving about 1 inch uncut at each end. Pry open the cut part of the peel.

❷ For each boat, scoop out the banana pulp and mix with 1/2 cup whipped topping and 1 tablespoon peanuts.

❸ Stuff banana mixture back into the peel, and top with a cherry.

Apple Boats

Sandwich-style cheese slices (3)

Apples (3)

1/2 cup peanut butter

1/4 cup chopped peanuts

1/4 cup crispy rice cereal

1/4 cup raisins

Toothpicks (6)

❶ Cut cheese slices in half diagonally.

❷ Cut apples in half and core. Scoop out the middle of apples, chop, and mix with remaining ingredients. Stuff apple shells with the mixture.

❸ Thread a toothpick through each slice of cheese "sail," and stick into the apple "boats."

Tuna Tug Boats

Green pepper (1)

6-oz. can tuna fish

1/4 cup mayonnaise

*Sandwich-style cheese
   slice (1)*

Toothpicks (2)

❶ Cut green pepper in half, and discard seeds and membrane.

❷ Mix tuna fish with mayonnaise. Stuff mixture into green pepper "boats."

❸ Cut cheese "sail" in half diagonally. Insert toothpick through cheese and into green pepper.

Spud Boats

Large baking potatoes (2)

1/8 cup milk

1/4 cup grated cheese

Sandwich-style cheese slice
   (1)

Toothpicks (2)

❶ Bake the potatoes. Slice each along the top, leaving about 1 inch uncut at each end. Pry open the cut part, and remove pulp.

❷ Mash the pulp with the milk and cheese.

❸ Stuff mixture back into "boats."

❹ Cut cheese slice in half diagonally. Thread a toothpick through each slice of cheese "sail," and stick into the spud "boats."

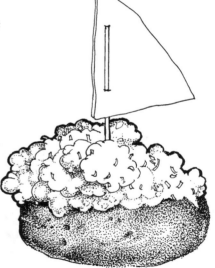

Carousels

Large apple (1)

2 tablespoons peanut butter

Small animal crackers (8)

Pretzel sticks (8)

Large gumdrops (2)

❶ Core the apple, and slice into 6 rounds. Discard top and bottom round.

❷ For each carousel, spread 1 apple slice with peanut butter. Stand 4 animal crackers in peanut butter around edges of apple. Insert 4 pretzel sticks, evenly spaced, into apple. Push the second apple slice into top of pretzel sticks, and add gumdrop over top hole.

CHAPTER 3

Play with Your Food

Involving children in the preparation of a snack will make them more interested in eating it. This chapter contains recipes that are as much fun to make as to eat. So let your children make their own snacks from this chapter—they're sure to love them.

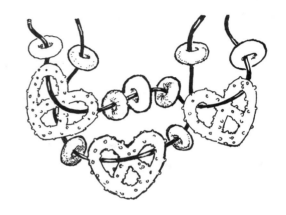

Painted Toast

8 tablespoons milk

Food coloring

White sandwich bread
   (4 slices)

❶ Place 2 tablespoons milk in 4 separate containers. Add a few drops of food coloring to each, making each cup a different color. Stir.

❷ Using clean paintbrushes, paint designs on the bread. Toast in a toaster.

Dominos

Graham crackers (4)

1/2 cup ready-made white frosting

Black shoestring licorice (16 1-inch pieces)

1/8 cup mini chocolate chips

❶ Divide each graham cracker along ridges, into 4 small rectangles. Frost each with white frosting.

❷ Place 1 piece of licorice in the center of each rectangle, dividing the rectangles in half.

❸ On each side of the licorice, place upside down chocolate chips (any number of them from 0 to 6) into the frosting to create numbers on the dominos.

Alphabites

1 tube refrigerated dinner
  rolls* (8 count)

1 egg white

Food coloring

*Frozen bread dough (thawed)
  may be substituted

❶ Roll each dough piece between hands until long and narrow. Form into letter of the alphabet. Place letters 2 inches apart on ungreased cookie sheet.

❷ Mix a few drops of food coloring with the egg white, and paint the mixture onto the dough letters. Bake about 14 minutes at 375°F.

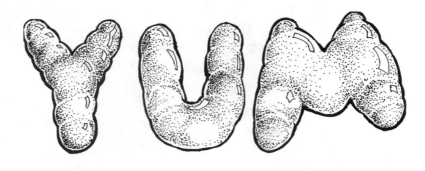

Alphacakes

2 cups baking mix

2 eggs

1 cup milk

❶ Mix all ingredients together. Using a spoon, drizzle batter in heated pan to form a letter. (Make it backwards.) When it has browned on one side, pour an additional 1/4 cup batter over the top of the letter. Cook until brown, and flip over to cook the other side.

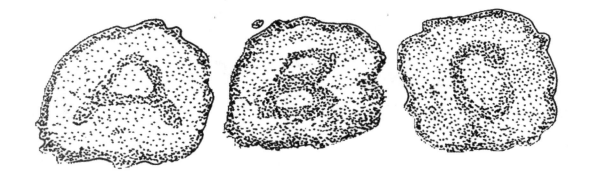

Peanut Butter Play Dough

1 cup creamy peanut butter

1 cup light corn syrup

1 1/2 cups dry milk

1 1/2 cups powdered sugar

❶ Mix all ingredients together and knead slightly. Play . . . and eat!

Cheesy Shapes

MAKES 18

2 cups cheddar cheese,
   shredded

1 1/3 cups flour

8 tablespoons butter,
   softened

1 teaspoon baking powder

❶ Mix all ingredients until well combined. Roll out the dough on floured surface. Cut with cookie cutters, and place on an ungreased cookie sheet. Bake for 10 minutes at 400°F. Cool.

Toast Cutouts

Sandwich bread (4 slices)

1/4 cup peanut butter

1/4 cup jelly

❶ Toast bread. Spread peanut butter on 2 slices of toast and jelly on the other 2 slices. Using the same cookie cutter, cut out centers of each piece of toast. Place jelly cutouts into centers of peanut butter toast and peanut butter cutouts into centers of jelly toasts.

Happy Apples

Medium red apple (1)

3 tablespoons peanut butter

Mini marshmallows (16–24)

❶ Core and cut apples into 8 slices.

❷ Spread peanut butter on top of each slice of apple.

❸ Place marshmallow "teeth" on top of 4 of the apple slices, peanut butter side up, then top with the other apple slices, peanut butter side down.

Volcanos

Sugar cones (2)

Caramels (2)

1/4 cup chocolate chips

Marshmallows (2)

❶ Stand each cone upright in a microwave-safe cup.

❷ Place 1 unwrapped caramel and half of the chocolate chips in each cone. Microwave on high approximately 15 seconds.

❸ Place 1 marshmallow in each cone, and microwave an additional 10–15 seconds or until marshmallow "volcano" rises above the edges of the cone.

❹ Cool for approximately 1 minute before eating.

Treat Necklaces

4-oz. package shoestring licorice

4 cups various candy, cereal, pretzels, etc., with holes in the centers

❶ String licorice through snacks, and knot ends together.

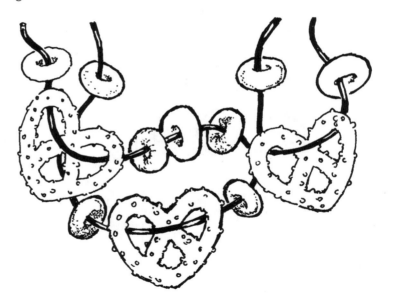

Sweet Flowers

Keebler Butter Cookies® (8)

Small gumdrops (16)

Lollipop sticks (8)

❶ For each flower, poke a lollipop stick through the top of 1 gumdrop, and move it 1 inch down the stick.

❷ Place 1 Keebler Butter Cookie® and another gumdrop right side up on the stick, making sure that the gumdrops hold the cookie securely in place.

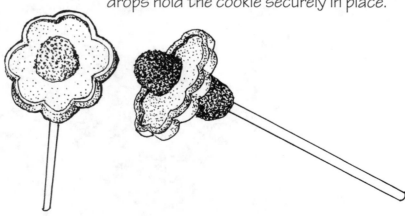

CHAPTER 4
Holiday Snacks

Holiday memories often include the special foods we share. These recipes are sure to be favorites with kids on those special days. So make a treat and a tradition!

Heart Cupcakes

18.25-oz. cake mix, any flavor

16-oz. tub ready-made white frosting, tinted pink with red food coloring, if desired

Decorator sprinkles or decorator frosting

❶ Prepare cake mix as directed on package. Line 36 cupcake tins with paper liners. Pour batter into liners, filling each only 1/2 full.

❷ Place a small marble between each liner and tin. (This will create the heart shape.) Bake as directed for cupcakes, shortening cooking time slightly. Cool. Remove marbles.

❸ Frost cupcakes, and decorate as desired.

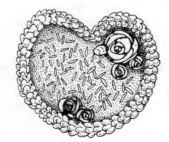

Cupid's Hearts

MAKES 12

Large pretzel knots (12)

Pretzel sticks (12)

1 cup pink or red chocolate candy wafers, for melting

Large candy conversation hearts (12)

Red shoestring licorice (36 1/2-inch pieces)

❶ Lay pretzel knots on waxed paper. Melt chocolate wafers, and pour carefully into the 3 "holes" of each pretzel.

❷ Break each pretzel stick in half, placing 1 half into chocolate in top right "hole" and the other half into chocolate in top left "hole" in line with each other.

❸ Freeze for 15 minutes or until chocolate is hardened. Using remaining chocolate as "glue," place conversation hearts on upside down at end of top right pretzel stick. Freeze again for 1 minute to set chocolate.

❹ Again using melted chocolate, place 3 pieces of licorice at ends of each pretzel stick on the left. Freeze for 1 minute.

Pots O' Gold

1/4 cup butter or margarine

3 cups mini marshmallows

Green food coloring

4 cups Cheerios® cereal

Black shoestring licorice
(9 6-inch pieces)

Gold foil-covered chocolate
coins (about 45)

❶ Melt butter or margarine in saucepan over low heat. Add marshmallows, and stir until melted. Remove from heat.

❷ Stir in several drops of green food coloring. Add Cheerios®. Stir until well mixed.

❸ Spray muffin tins with non-stick cooking spray. Divide cereal mixture between 9 muffin tins, and form into "pots," bringing cereal mixture up higher than the sides of the tins.

❹ Stick in licorice "handles." Cool. Remove from tins. Add chocolate coins.

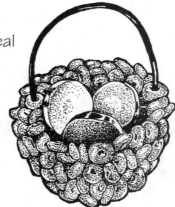

The Best Nests

4 cups mini marshmallows

3 tablespoons butter

6 cups crispy rice cereal

1/2 cup shredded sweetened
   coconut

Green food coloring

1/2 cup jelly beans

Chick-shaped
   marshmallows (24)

❶ Melt marshmallows and butter over low heat. Remove from heat, and stir in cereal. Spray 24 muffin cups with cooking spray. Mold cereal mixture into muffin cups, shaping into nests.

❷ Mix coconut with several drops of food coloring. Fill each nest with green coconut, jelly beans, and a chick.

Hidden Egg Cupcakes

18.25-oz. cake mix, any flavor

Small foil-wrapped chocolate
   eggs (24)

16-oz. tub ready-made
   frosting

❶ Line 24 muffin tins with baking cup liners. Prepare cake mix as directed on package.

❷ Fill 1/3 of each muffin tin with batter and place 1 unwrapped chocolate egg on top. Add additional batter until muffin cup is 2/3 full.

❸ Bake for 20 minutes at 350°F. When cool, frost and decorate as desired.

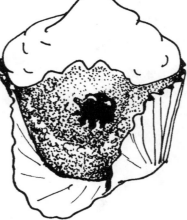

Bunny Cupcakes

MAKES 24

18.25-oz. cake mix, any flavor

16-oz. tub ready-made white frosting

Red food coloring

1 cup shredded coconut

Keebler Vienna Fingers® cookies (48)

Red Hots® cinnamon candies (48)

Pink jelly beans (24)

Red shoestring licorice (96 1-inch pieces)

Mini marshmallows (48)

❶ Prepare cake mix as directed on package. Pour into muffin tins lined with paper baking cups. Bake as directed. Cool.

❷ Using a few drops of red food coloring, tint 1/3 cup of frosting. Frost the centers of 1 side of each cookie with pink frosting. Set aside.

❸ Frost cupcakes with remaining white frosting. Sprinkle coconut evenly over tops of cupcakes.

❹ For each cupcake, attach 2 Keebler Vienna Fingers® cookie "ears," 2 Red Hots® cinnamon candy "eyes," 1 jelly bean "nose," 4 licorice "whiskers," and 2 marshmallow "teeth."

Bunny Buns

7.5-oz. package of 10
   refrigerated biscuits

1/2 cup raisins

1/4 cup flaked coconut

❶ Place 5 whole biscuits on greased cookie sheet. Cut remaining 5 biscuits in half, and place as "ears" at top of whole biscuits.

❷ Add raisin "eyes," "noses," and "mouths," and add coconut "whiskers."

❸ Bake for 10 minutes at 425°F.

Easter Basket Cupcakes

18.25-oz. cake mix, any flavor

16-oz. tub ready-made frosting

Shoestring licorice (24 7-inch pieces)

1/2 cup shredded, sweetened coconut

Green food coloring

1/2 cup mini jelly beans

❶ Prepare cake mix as directed on package. Pour into muffin tins lined with paper baking cups. Bake as directed. Frost when cool.

❷ For each cupcake, place a piece of licorice into each side, poking down into the cake to secure.

❸ Tint coconut with several drops of food coloring. Sprinkle coconut on top of each cupcake, and add jelly bean "eggs."

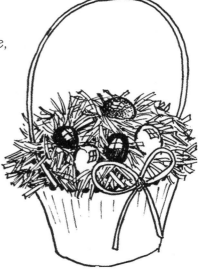

Easter Bonnets

Nilla® wafers (12)

Large round sugar cookies (12)

Decorator frosting in a tube

❶ Spread a small amount of decorator frosting on the bottom of each small cookie, and press them onto the centers of the large cookies to adhere.

❷ Using the decorator frosting, create a ribbon and bow around the edge of the small cookie. Decorate the rest of the bonnet as desired.

Firecrackers

3-oz. paper cups (8)

1 cup blue fruit juice drink

1 cup white fruit juice drink

Popsicle sticks (8)

*Shoestring licorice
   (8 4-inch pieces)*

1 cup red fruit juice drink

❶ Fill each cup 1/3 full with blue drink. Freeze until firm.

❷ Repeat the procedure with white drink, inserting a popsicle stick and licorice piece when firm but not solid.

❸ Fill each cup with red drink. Freeze until hard. Peel paper cup away to eat.

Boo Pops

Round lollipops (10)

Circular-shaped Fruit Roll
Ups® (10)

Shoestring licorice
(10 10-inch pieces)

Decorator frosting in a tube

❶ Fold 1 unwrapped Fruit Roll Up® around lollipop.

❷ Tie 1 piece of licorice around the base of the lollipop.
Add "eyes" with decorator frosting.

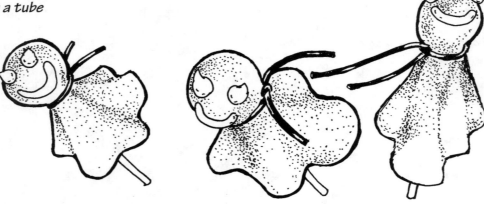

Scarecrow

*Chocolate foil-wrapped candy
    with a face on it (available
    at Halloween) (1)*

*Snack size package of
    candy (1)*

Tootsie Rolls® (2)

*Sweet and sour candy
    rolls (2)*

*Shoestring licorice
    (1 8-inch piece)*

❶ Using a hot glue gun, glue chocolate "head" to candy package.

❷ Glue on wrapped Tootsie Roll® "arms" and sweet and sour candy roll "legs."

❸ Tie waist with licorice.

Black Cat Cupcakes

18.25-oz. cake mix, any flavor

16-oz. tub ready-made
chocolate frosting

Keebler Snackin' Grahams®
(48)

Black shoestring licorice
(144 1-inch pieces)

Brown or pink M & M®
candies (24)

Green M & M® candies (48)

Yellow snowflake decorator
sprinkles (48)

1 cup mini chocolate chips

❶ Prepare cake mix as directed on package. Pour into muffin tins lined with paper baking cups. Bake as directed. Frost when cool.

❷ For each cupcake, attach 2 Snackin' Graham® "ears" and 2 green M & M® "eyes." Using frosting as adhesive, place a yellow snowflake sprinkle in the center of each "eye."

❸ Use 1 brown M & M® for a nose and 6 pieces of licorice for whiskers. Place chocolate chips over remaining areas.

Gobble Up a Gobbler

Chocolate striped cookies (9)

Caramels (6)

Candy corn (6)

❶ Cut 3 cookies in half through vertical chocolate stripes. In the same direction, cut 1/4 off the remaining 6 cookies.

❷ Place 6 unwrapped caramels approximately 3 inches apart on cookie sheet covered with aluminum foil. Place in a warm oven just until caramels start to soften. Spread out softened caramels slightly, forming into turkey body shapes. Stand one 3/4 cookie up on cut edge in the caramel. Directly in front of it stand one 1/2 cookie on edge. Place 1 candy corn "turkey beak" in the caramel in front.

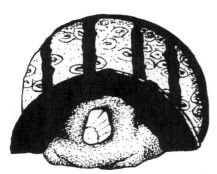

Fantail Turkeys

Oreo® cookies (8)

Large malted milk balls (8)

1/4 cup chocolate ready-
made frosting

Candy corn (50–60)

❶ Pry open each cookie into a 90° angle. Place a malted milk ball between the 2 halves of each cookie.

❷ Using frosting as adhesive, place a candy corn "beak" on each malted milk ball "body," and 5–6 candy corn "tail feathers" around the edges of each raised cookie half.

Mini Cornucopias

Cone-shaped corn snacks
*   such as Bugles® (20)*

2 tablespoons peanut butter

1/2 cup fruit-shaped cereal
*   such as Trix®*

❶ Place a small amount of peanut butter in each Bugle®. Put cereal into the peanut butter.

Indian Sweet Corn

1 cup sugar

1/2 cup corn syrup

2 tablespoons butter

8 cups popped corn

1 cup nuts (peanuts, pecans, or almonds)

3/4 cup dried fruit bits

Yellow plastic wrap

❶ Mix sugar, corn syrup, and butter together over medium heat. Bring to a boil and stir until sugar dissolves.

❷ Mix popcorn, nuts, and fruit together. Pour sugar syrup over the popcorn mixture, and stir well. Place in a roasting pan, and bake for 1 hour at 250°F, stirring occasionally.

❸ Shape warm popcorn mixture into corncob shapes, and wrap with yellow plastic wrap.

Cracker Houses

Large graham cracker rectangles (15)

3 egg whites at room temperature

1/2 teaspoon cream of tartar

3 cups powdered sugar

8" X 8" pieces of cardboard covered with foil (5)

16-oz. tub white ready-made frosting

Various candy, cookies for decorating

❶ Break graham crackers into squares. Mix together egg whites, cream of tartar, and powdered sugar. Fasten the walls (4 cracker squares) onto the foil with blobs of egg white mixture. Repeat the process for the 2 square roof pieces, creating an A-frame roof. (Note: ends of roof will be open.) Let harden overnight.

❷ When dry, attach candy and cookie decorations with tub frosting.

Tree Cones

1 cup white chocolate chips

Green food coloring

Sugar cones (4)

*Decorator frosting and
    candies*

❶ Melt chocolate chips over low heat. Tint with a few drops of green food coloring. Spread on cones until covered.

❷ Decorate trees with candies and frosting.

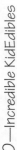

Stained Glass Ornaments

MAKES 4

Brightly colored hard candy, such as Life Savers® (30–50 depending on size of cookie cutters)

Cookie cutters (4)

Decorator sprinkles

Shoestring licorice (4 10-inch pieces)

❶ On a baking sheet, place cookie cutters on small pieces of foil, wrapping edges of foil up around edges of cookie cutters. Spray with nonstick cooking spray. Fill each cookie cutter with crushed, unwrapped hard candies.

❷ Bake at 350°F until melted, about 10–12 minutes. Immediately add decorator sprinkles. Use a toothpick to create a hole near the top.

❸ When cool, remove candy from cookie cutter and string licorice through the hole for hanging.

Rudolphs

Large pretzel knots (24)

1 cup chocolate chips

Pretzel sticks (96)

Red M & M® candies (24)

Green M & M® candies (48)

❶ Lay pretzel knots on waxed paper.

❷ Melt chocolate, and pour carefully into the 3 "holes" of each pretzel.

❸ Add 4 pretzel stick "antlers," 2 green candy "eyes" and 1 red candy "nose" to each reindeer.

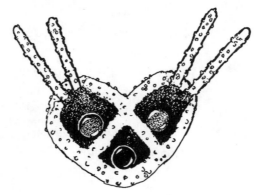

Holiday Yule Logs

Sandwich bread (4 slices)

1/4 cup peanut butter

1/4 cup jelly

*1/2 cup chocolate ready-
   made frosting*

❶ Remove crusts from bread.

❷ With a rolling pin, flatten bread. Spread peanut butter and jelly on top.

❸ Roll the bread up, and frost the outside with frosting.

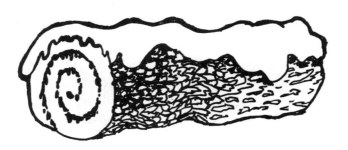

Graham Cracker Sleds

2 graham crackers

5 candy canes

2 large pretzel knots, or pretzel-shaped cookies

Red shoestring licorice (2 9-inch pieces)

1 tablespoon ready-made frosting, any flavor

Decorator frosting

❶ Lay graham crackers across glasses or mugs to elevate. Spread a thin line of frosting down each long side of graham crackers. Place a candy cane along each side, securing in frosting so that the curved ends go down over the edge of the crackers.

❷ Using a serrated knife, cut off the curve of the remaining candy cane, and then cut the remaining straight part into 2 equal pieces. Again using frosting, glue straight pieces of candy cane onto cracker between the curved ends of the other candy canes. Leave as much as possible of the straight candy cane extending over edge of cracker.

❸ Glue licorice piece onto each side of cracker next to the curves of the 2 candy canes. Let frosting harden for at least 2 hours. When frosting is dry and candy canes are firmly attached, invert the graham crackers.

❹ Using frosting, attach pretzel at the end of the straight piece of candy cane. Let harden. Decorate with decorator frosting.

Snow Nuts

*Full-size powdered sugar
    doughnuts (4)*

*Mini powdered sugar
    doughnuts (4)*

*Powdered sugar doughnut
    holes (4)*

Pretzel sticks (8)

Large gumdrops (4)

Decorator frosting

❶ Arrange doughnuts, placing large on bottom to small on top. Secure with toothpicks if necessary.

❷ Place pretzel sticks in sides for arms. Decorate face, and attach gumdrop hats with frosting.

Snow Balls

1/2 gallon ice cream, any flavor

1 cup chopped candy or nuts

❶ Scoop ice cream into 1/2-cup-sized balls. Roll in chopped candy and nuts.

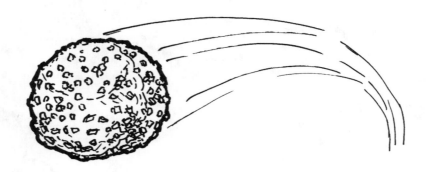

Christmas Angel

Sugar cone (1)

Large pretzel knot (1)

*2 tablespoons vanilla
frosting*

*Decorator sprinkles or
colored sugar*

Round lollipop (1)

Life Saver® (1)

❶ Cut 1/2 inch off the point of the sugar cone. Frost the cone and pretzel, and roll in sugar or sprinkles.

❷ Push lollipop stick into point of cone. Using frosting as adhesive, attach pretzel "wings" and Life Saver® "halo." Add frosting "eyes" and "mouth" if desired.

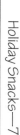

Little Drummers

Double Stuff Oreo®
  cookies (8)

1/2 cup ready-made white
  frosting

Fruit by the Foot® fruit roll (1)

Red shoestring licorice
  (40 1-inch pieces)

Black shoestring licorice
  (8 2-inch pieces)

Small gumdrops (8)

❶ For each Little Drummer, place 2 Oreo® cookies together using a small amount of frosting as adhesive and frost top and sides.

❷ Cut two 6-inch strips of Fruit by the Foot® fruit roll. Cut 4 long strips of equal size from each 6-inch strip. Wrap 1 strip around the top and 1 strip around the bottom of each "drum."

❸ Place 10 red shoestring licorice pieces in a zigzag pattern between the fruit roll strips on each "drum."

❹ Stick 1 piece of black licorice into the base of each gumdrop "drumstick." Lay "drumsticks" on top of drums.

Holly Berry Wreaths

4 cups mini marshmallows

1/3 cup butter or margarine

Green food coloring

3 cups cornflakes

Red Hots® cinnamon candies

❶ Melt butter or margarine in saucepan over low heat. Add marshmallows, and stir until melted. Remove from heat.

❷ Stir in several drops of green food coloring. Add cereal. Stir until well mixed.

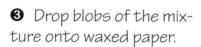

❸ Drop blobs of the mixture onto waxed paper.

❹ Spray hands with nonstick cooking spray. Shape cornflake mixture into wreaths. Add Red Hots® candy "berries." Cool.

Holiday Wreath

Red shoestring licorice
(1 15-inch piece)

Green Life Savers® (13)

❶ String Life Savers® on licorice. Tie ends of licorice into a bow, creating a wreath.

CHAPTER 5

Party Snacks

What is a party without food? Definitely not a party! The snacks in this chapter are sure to be a hit with kids of all ages. They are certainly not the same old cupcakes as usual. They are unique, memorable, delicious, and best of all . . . easy!

Ice Cream Wheelies

Large round cookies, any kind (12)

2 cups ice cream, any flavor

1/2 cup decorator sprinkles

❶ For each wheelie, put 1/3 cup of softened ice cream between 2 cookies.

❷ Place sprinkles in shallow dish. Roll ice cream wheelies in sprinkles, coating all around.

❸ Freeze for 1 hour or until firm.

Yo-Yos

Nilla® wafers (24)

1 1/2 cups ice cream, any flavor

12 strands shoestring licorice

❶ Scoop 1/8 cup softened ice cream onto bottom of 12 Nilla® wafers. Top with remaining cookies, sandwiching ice cream in between.

❷ Tie a knot at the bottom of each licorice strand. Poke other end of licorice into ice cream in each yo-yo.

❸ Freeze at least 30 minutes.

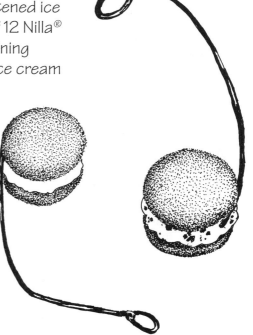

Smilies

18.25-oz. cake mix, any flavor

16-oz. tub ready-made white frosting

Yellow food coloring

Junior Mints® (48)

Black shoestring licorice (24 2-inch pieces and 48 1/2-inch pieces)

❶ Prepare cake mix as directed on package. Pour into muffin tins lined with paper baking cups. Bake as directed. Cool.

❷ Tint frosting a bright yellow with several drops of food coloring. Frost cupcakes. Place 2 Junior Mint® "eyes" on each cupcake. Using one 2-inch piece and two 1/2-inch pieces of licorice, place "smiles" on each cupcake.

Pizza Cookies

18-oz. refrigerated sugar
  cookie dough

16-oz. tub ready-made white
  frosting

Red food coloring

Red Fruit Roll-Up® (1)

1/4 cup flour

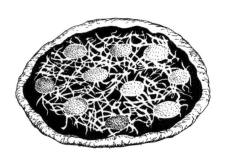

❶ Spread flour on working surface. Roll out cookie dough to a circle with 13-inch diameter. Place on cookie sheet, and bake at 350°F for 11–13 minutes. Cool.

❷ With the food coloring, tint half the frosting red. Spread the red frosting over cookie.

❸ Spoon the remaining white frosting into a decorating bag with round decorating tip (or put frosting in a sandwich bag and snip off one corner). Squeeze out short spurts of frosting "cheese" onto the red "pizza sauce."

❹ Unroll the fruit roll, and cut 1-inch diameter circles from it. Lay the fruit roll "pepperoni" onto the pizza.

Caramel Apple Heads

14-oz. package caramels

Popsicle sticks (6)

Apples (6)

Candies, nuts, and cereal for
decoration

❶ Melt caramels over low heat.

❷ Poke popsicle sticks into base
of apples. Swirl apples in caramel,
spreading evenly over apples.
Let excess caramel drip off.
Place apples on waxed paper.

❸ Decorate to look like
people while caramel is still
warm.

Crunchy Fruit Cones

Waffle cones (4)

1/3 cup melted chocolate

Decorator sprinkles

2 cups cut up fruit

1/4 cup granola

❶ Dip tops of cones into chocolate and then into sprinkles. Let cool.

❷ Fill cones with fruit, and sprinkle with granola. Serve immediately.

Teddy Bear Turn-A-Rounds

Teddy Grahams (25)

Life Savers® candies (10)

Lollipop or popsicle sticks (5)

❶ For each lollipop place 5 Teddy Grahams on cookie sheet in circular shape so feet almost touch. Place 2 Life Savers® in a plastic bag, and crush. Pour candy pieces in center hole of crackers making sure to catch all feet in the candy. Insert a stick between 2 crackers and into candy.

❷ Place in a 250°F oven for 5 minutes or until candy is melted. Cool.

Cookies on a Stick

17.5-oz. package dry cookie
  mix

1 egg

1/4 cup oil

1 tablespoon water

Popsicle sticks (24)

Decorator frosting

Candies

❶ Stir together first 4 ingredients. Shape into 1-1/2-inch balls, and lay approximately 2 inches apart on cookie sheet.

❷ Insert a popsicle stick into each ball and flatten dough slightly. Bake for 12–14 minutes at 375°F. Let cool before removing from cookie sheet. Decorate with frosting and candies.

Clown-A-Rounds

1 quart ice cream, any flavor

Large circular or flower-shaped cookies (8)

Sugar cones (8)

Decorator candies and frosting

❶ Place a scoop of ice cream on top of each cookie.

❷ Place inverted cone "hat" on top of ice cream.

❸ Use candies to decorate with a clown face.

Creative Cones

Sugar or waffle cones (6)

1/2 cup melted chocolate

Assorted sprinkles, chopped nuts, or chopped candy

Ice cream, any flavor

❶ Dip tops of cones in chocolate and then immediately in candy or nuts. Cool on waxed paper.

❷ Fill with ice cream, and enjoy.

Ice Cream Cone Cupcakes

18.25-oz. cake mix, any flavor

Plain ice cream cones (24)

16-oz. tub ready-made frosting

Decorator sprinkles (optional)

❶ Prepare cake mix as directed on package. Stand cones up in muffin tins. Fill cones 1/2 full with batter. Bake as directed. Cool, frost, and decorate.

Pudding Cones

Small box instant pudding
   mix, any flavor

2 cups milk

Plain ice cream cones (6)

Canned dairy whipped topping

Decorator sprinkles

❶ Combine pudding mix and cold milk. Beat for 2 minutes. Let stand for 5 minutes.

❷ Spoon pudding into ice cream cones. Cover cones with foil, and freeze until firm, about 2 hours.

❸ Right before serving, top cones with whipped topping and sprinkles.

Flower Pots

Cupcakes baked in ice cream cones (24) (see page 92)

16-oz. tub chocolate ready-made frosting

1 cup shredded coconut

Green food coloring

Lollipop sticks (24)

Sandwich cookies (24)

16-oz. tub white ready-made frosting

Assorted small candies

❶ Frost the cupcakes with the chocolate frosting.

❷ Tint coconut with a few drops of green food coloring. Mix well, and sprinkle on top of frosted cupcakes.

❸ Insert a lollipop stick between the halves of each cookie. Cover front and back of each cookie with white frosting, and decorate with candies to create the petals of flowers.

Dandy Sand

16-oz. package vanilla
    sandwich cookies

2 cups milk

3.4-oz. box vanilla instant
    pudding

8-oz. tub whipped topping,
    thawed

10-oz. clear plastic cups (8)

Decorative candies

❶ Crush sandwich cookies. Set aside.

❷ Combine pudding mix and milk. Mix as directed on package. Chill for 5 minutes.

❸ Stir whipped topping and half of the crushed cookies into the pudding.

❹ Fill each cup with layers of crushed cookie, pudding mixture, and more crushed cookie. Place in refrigerator for approximately 1 hour. Decorate.

Watermelon Ice Cream

1/2 gallon green ice cream or sherbet

1 pint vanilla ice cream

1/2 cup chocolate chips

2 pints pink ice cream or sherbet

❶ Soften green ice cream. Cover all sides of a 3-quart bowl with plastic wrap. Press green ice cream into bowl, creating a 1-inch lining all over. Freeze until firm.

❷ Spoon softened vanilla ice cream over green ice cream, and freeze until hardened.

❸ Mix chocolate chips with softened pink ice cream or sherbet. Spread in bowl on top of vanilla ice cream. Cover with foil and freeze.

❹ To serve, soften slightly and remove from bowl by pulling on plastic wrap. Invert, and remove plastic.

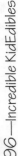

Hamburger Cookies

1/4 cup flaked coconut

Green food coloring

Red gumdrops (3)

Nilla® wafers (6)

Miniature peppermint
    patties (3)

1/2 teaspoon sesame seeds

Honey

❶ Tint coconut with a few drops of food coloring.

❷ With rolling pin, roll out gumdrops until flat. Cut 2 dime-sized circles from each.

❸ To assemble each hamburger, place 1 wafer upside down on plate. Place peppermint on top. Add coconut "lettuce" and gumdrop "tomato." Top with another wafer. Attach sesame seeds with very small amounts of honey.

Popcorn Cake

5 oz. unpopped corn (about
    15 cups popped)

5 oz. small gumdrops

5 oz. cocktail peanuts

12 oz. marshmallows

1/3 cup butter or margarine

❶ Pop the corn, and stir together with gumdrops and peanuts.

❷ Melt marshmallows with butter, and pour over popcorn mixture. Press into a greased angel food cake pan. Cool. Invert, and cut to serve.

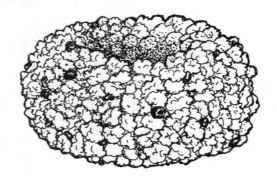

Special Gelatin

6-oz. package gelatin

5-oz. clear plastic cups (8)

6 oz. gummi candies or fruit snacks

❶ Prepare gelatin as directed on package. Pour into clear plastic cups. Chill.

❷ When partially set, add gummi candies, and refrigerate until firm. Eat right away as some candies may get mushy.

FUN IDEAS:

Blue gelatin with gummi fish

Red gelatin with hearts

Orange gelatin with gummi spiders or worms

Magic Wands

1 cup chocolate chips

Large pretzel sticks (24)

*Decorator sprinkles, chopped
    candy or nuts*

❶ Melt chocolate chips over low heat.

❷ Dip half of each pretzel into melted chocolate and then into sprinkles, candy, or nuts. Place on waxed paper to cool.

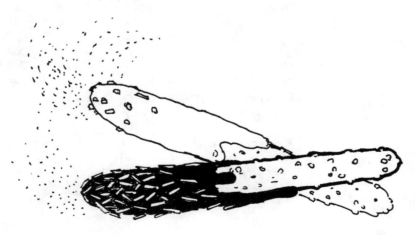

Pop Tops

Decorator sprinkles

3-oz. paper cups (10)

Small box instant pudding
  mix, any flavor

2 cups milk, or chocolate milk

Popsicle sticks (10)

❶ Shake sprinkles into bottoms of the cups.

❶ Prepare pudding as directed on package. Spoon pudding into cups, and cover with foil.

❶ Using a sharp knife, make a small slit in the center of foil, and slide a popsicle stick through the slit and into the pudding in each cup. Put cups in the freezer for about 5 hours. To serve, remove foil and paper cup from each pop.

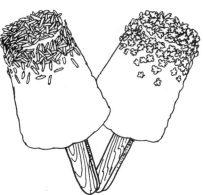

Sunshines

17.5-oz. Betty Crocker Sugar
  Cookie Mix®

1/2 cup margarine or butter,
  melted

1 egg

Bugles® corn snacks (144)

16-oz. tub ready-made white
  frosting (2)

Yellow food coloring

Yellow crystal decorator
  sugar

❶ Combine the first 3 ingredients. Drop by rounded tablespoons onto cookie sheets. Insert 6 Bugles® into each cookie dough ball. Flatten dough slightly.

❷ Bake for 10–12 minutes at 375°F or just until the cookie dough begins to brown. Let cool.

❸ Tint frosting a bright yellow with several drops of food coloring. Frost Bugles® corn snacks and tops of cookies with yellow frosting. Sprinkle with decorator sugar.

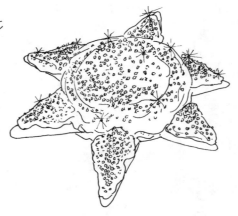

CHAPTER 6

Fun, Quick, and Easy

Not every day is a party, a holiday, or a day you have lots of time to spare, but every day your children will want a snack. This chapter is chock full of quick and easy yet delicious, enticing, and irresistible snacks.

Banana Bumps

1/4 cup chocolate chips

2 tablespoons peanut butter

1 banana

1/2 cup flaked coconut,
    chopped nuts, or crushed
    cereal

❶ Melt chocolate chips over low heat or in microwave. Stir in peanut butter.

❷ Peel banana, and cut into 1-inch pieces.

❸ Dip each piece into chocolate mixture and then into coconut, nuts, or cereal. Coat all sides. Lay on waxed paper to harden.

Banana Blankets

1 tablespoon sugar

1 teaspoon cinnamon

Sandwich bread (2 slices)

Banana (1)

1 tablespoon melted butter

❶ Mix together cinnamon and sugar.

❷ Remove crusts from bread. With a rolling pin, flatten bread.

❸ Cut banana in half, placing 1 half in each bread slice. Roll up tightly.

❹ Spread melted butter and cinnamon sugar over each rolled bread slice. Bake for 15 minutes at 400°F.

Tortilla Wheels

Large burrito-size tortillas
   (2)

1/4 cup soft cream cheese

Thin slices ham (6)

Sandwich-style American
   cheese (6 slices)

1/4 cup grated carrot

❶ Spread 1/8 cup cream cheese on each tortilla. Top with sliced ham and cheese. Sprinkle grated carrot over the top. Roll up each tortilla tightly, and cut each crosswise into 6 slices.

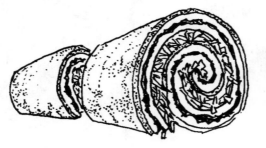
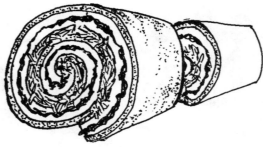

Bird Nests

Large shredded wheat biscuits (3)

1/2 cup shredded coconut

1 tablespoon brown sugar

1 teaspoon cinnamon

1/3 cup margarine or butter, melted

1 cup blueberries, grapes, or small melon balls

❶ Crumble shredded wheat into large bowl. Add coconut, brown sugar, cinnamon, and melted margarine or butter. Mix well.

❷ Line 6 muffin tins with liners. Divide mixture between muffin cups. Press into bottoms and up sides.

❸ Cook at 350°F for 8 minutes. Cool. Remove liners, and fill with fruit "eggs."

Looking Glass Cookies

**18-oz. tube refrigerated
sugar cookie dough**

Life Savers® candy rolls (2)

❶ Freeze tube of cookie dough for 30 minutes. Slice dough into 1/4-inch slices, and place on cookie sheet.

❷ Using a miniature cookie cutter, cut out the centers of each slice.

❸ Crush 1–2 Life Savers® candies per cookie, and pour into cut-out area of cookie dough slices.

❹ Bake at 350°F for 11–13 minutes. Cool. Carefully remove from cookie sheets while still slightly warm.

Dinosaur Eggs

MAKES 6

6 eggs

1 tablespoon vinegar

Red food coloring

15-oz. jar beets (2)

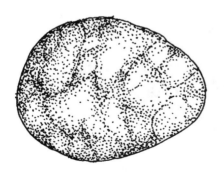

❶ Place eggs in a saucepan, and cover with cold water. Cover pan, and bring water to a boil. Remove pan from heat, and keep covered for 15 minutes. Cool eggs in cold water. Tap shells with a metal spoon until they are cracked all over. Do not peel. Place eggs in a bowl.

❷ Pour vinegar, several drops of food coloring, and liquid from beets into a saucepan. Bring to a boil. Pour over eggs, and cover. Refrigerate for several hours.

❸ Peel eggs to serve.

S'Morp

2 1/2 cups Golden Grahams
   cereal

1 cup peanuts

1 cup mini marshmallows

1/2 cup chocolate chips

❶ Mix all ingredients.

Gorp

1 cup Teddy Grahams

1 cup pretzel sticks

1 cup Ritz® Bits crackers

1 cup fish-shaped crackers

1/2 cup raisins

1/2 cup peanuts

❶ Mix all ingredients
(or any other combi-
nation of crackers,
cereal, nuts, etc.)

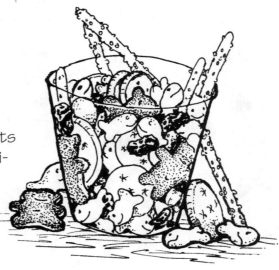

Hamburger Cups

1 lb. ground beef

1/2 cup barbecue sauce

7.5-oz. package of 10
   refrigerated biscuits

1/2 cup shredded cheddar
   cheese

❶ Brown ground beef, and drain.

❷ Stir in barbecue sauce. Heat until warm.

❸ Spray muffin tins with cooking spray. Press biscuit dough into muffin tins. Fill with meat mixture, and sprinkle with cheese.

❹ Bake for 10 minutes at 400°F.

One-Eyed Jack

Sandwich bread (4 slices)

1/4 cup butter

4 eggs

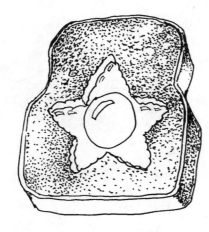

❶ Butter both sides of bread. Cut out centers of bread with a cookie cutter.

❷ Spray griddle with cooking spray. Heat over medium high heat. Place the outside of bread in heated pan. Crack an egg in the middle of cut-out area. Cook until first sides are brown. Flip, and continue cooking other sides until brown.

Fruity Popcorn

3 quarts popped corn

1 envelope unsweetened fruit
   drink mix

1 cup sugar

3/4 cup water

❶ Spread popped corn on a cookie sheet.

❷ Combine all ingredients except popcorn in a saucepan. Cook and stir over medium heat until sugar is dissolved. Bring to a boil, and cook until candy thermometer reaches 270°F. Pour over popped corn, and mix to coat evenly. Place in 250°F oven for 10–15 minutes.

Walking Apples

Large apples (3)

1/2 cup vanilla yogurt

2 tablespoons raisins

2 tablespoons chopped nuts

1/4 teaspoon cinnamon

❶ Core apples, leaving the bottom skin intact. Scoop out the inside of the apples. Finely chop.

❷ Add chopped apple to the remaining ingredients. Mix well. Spoon back into the hole, and take it with you on a walk.

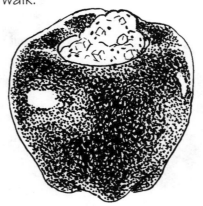

Orange Bowls

Oranges (4)

2 cups vanilla yogurt

1 cup raisins

❶ Cut off tops of oranges. Scoop out the pulp, and mash.

❷ Mix mashed pulp with yogurt and raisins, and stuff inside the orange peels.

Funky Monkey Bread

1 teaspoon cinnamon

1/4 cup sugar

7.5-oz. package of 10 refrig-
    erated biscuits

2 tablespoons butter, melted

1/2 cup brown sugar

❶ Combine cinnamon and sugar.

❷ Cut each biscuit into fourths. Roll each piece in cinnamon sugar. Place pieces evenly spaced in greased loaf pan.

❸ Mix brown sugar with melted butter, and pour over biscuits. Bake for 10–15 minutes at 350°F.

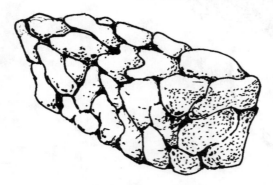

Fruit Dumplings

1 teaspoon cinnamon

2 tablespoons sugar

7.5-oz. package of 10 refrigerated biscuits

1 cup chunky applesauce

❶ Combine cinnamon and sugar.

❷ Flatten each biscuit into a 4-inch circle.
Place a spoonful of applesauce in the center of each.
Sprinkle with cinnamon sugar.

❸ Squeeze edges of biscuits together into a bundle.
Place each in a greased muffin tin.
Bake for 11 minutes
at 375°F.

Ham It Up in a Cup

Thin slices of ham (6)

6 eggs

1/2 cup shredded cheddar
cheese

❶ Grease 6 muffin cups. Fit 1 slice of ham around edges of each muffin cup.

❷ Break an egg into center of each, and top with cheese.

❸ Bake for 15–20 minutes at 375°F.

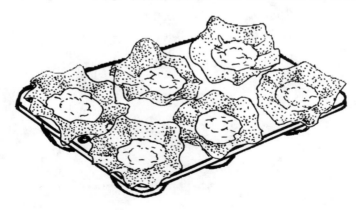

Banana Dogs

Hot dog buns (4)

1/2 cup peanut butter

Bananas (4)

*1/4 cup red jelly in squeeze
   container or pastry bag*

❶ Open hot dog buns.

❷ Spread each with peanut butter, and place a peeled banana inside.

❸ Squeeze jelly on top of each banana.

A Jumble of Crumble

1/2 cup light corn syrup

1/2 cup sugar

1 cup peanut butter

1 cup chow mein noodles

❶ Combine corn syrup and sugar. Bring to a boil over medium high heat.

❷ Remove from heat, and stir in peanut butter until mixture is smooth.

❸ Add chow mein noodles, and form into 1-inch balls.

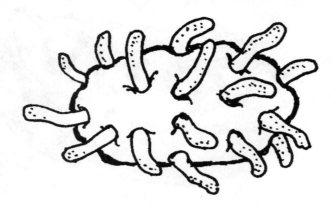

CHAPTER 7

IncrEdible Art

Yes, you could eat each and every one of the doughs, clays, putties, and paints in this chapter if you wanted to. They are not meant to be tasty, only safe and easy. Each recipe in this chapter is made from completely edible food items you probably already have in your cupboard. So don't worry. Get messy, create, and have fun!

Baking Soda Clay

2 cups baking soda

1 cup cornstarch

1 1/4 cups cold water

❶ Combine baking soda, cornstarch, and water in a saucepan. Stir until smooth.

❷ Cook over medium heat for 10–15 minutes, stirring constantly until mixture thickens. Turn out of pan, and cover with a damp cloth until cool.

❸ Knead until dough is smooth. Roll out to 1/4" thickness, and cut with cookie cutters. Using a toothpick, poke holes in the top of shapes for hanging.

❹ Air dry overnight, and decorate with paints or markers.

Flour Clay

4 cups flour

1 cup salt

1 1/2 cups water

❶ Combine all ingredients, stirring well. When well mixed, knead well.

❷ Form into shapes. Bake for approximately 1 hour at 350°F. Cool and paint.

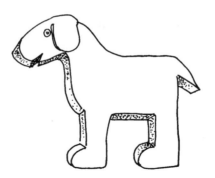

Slime

1 cup water

Food coloring

1 1/4 cups cornstarch

❶ Add food coloring to water until bright.

❷ Stir water into cornstarch, 1/4 cup at a time, until mixture flows without being runny. Play, and get messy!

Fruitie Tootie Putty

2 cups flour

3-oz. box sugar-free fruit-
    flavored gelatin

1 cup salt

4 tablespoons cream of
    tartar

2 tablespoons oil

2 cups boiling water

❶ Mix the first 4 ingredients together in a saucepan.

❷ Add oil and water, and stir over medium heat until it forms into a ball.

❸ Turn out onto waxed paper, and let cool. Store in airtight container.

Rainbow Goo

4 cups water

1 cup cornstarch

1/3 cup sugar

Food coloring

Sealable sandwich bags (5)

❶ Combine first 3 ingredients in a saucepan. Heat over medium heat, stirring frequently until mixture begins to thicken. Let stand in pan until cool.

❷ Divide into several containers. Add a different food coloring to each, and stir well.

❸ Place a spoonful of each colored mixture into a sealable bag. Knead until the mixture turns into a rainbow.

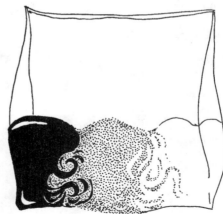

Pinch and Sniff Dough

MAKES ABOUT 5 CUPS

3 cups flour

1/2 cup salt

1 tablespoon alum

2 cups boiling water

2 envelopes unsweetened drink mix

3 tablespoons oil

Food coloring

❶ Combine flour, salt, and alum.

❷ In separate bowl, combine remaining ingredients, and then add to dry ingredients. Knead together, adding a little more flour if necessary. Store in airtight container.

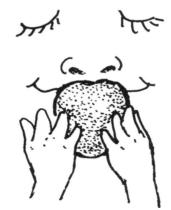

Play Dough (variation #1)

1 cup flour

1 cup salt

1 cup water

1 tablespoon cream of tartar

Food coloring

❶ Mix all ingredients together well. Store in airtight container.

Play Dough (variation #2)

2 1/2 cups flour

1/2 cup salt

3 tablespoons oil

1 1/2 cups boiling water

Food coloring

3 tablespoons alum

❶ Combine flour and salt.

❷ Add oil and boiling water mixed with several drops of food coloring.

❸ Add alum, and knead together.

❹ Store in airtight container.

Sparkly Dough

1 1/2 cups cold water

2 teaspoons food coloring

2 cups salt

1 cup cornstarch

❶ Combine water and food coloring in a pan.

❷ Add remaining ingredients. Cook over medium heat, stirring constantly until thickened (about 5 minutes). When cool enough to handle, knead for several minutes. Store in airtight container.

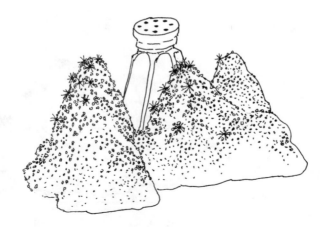

Finger Paint

2 cups boiling water

1/4 cup cornstarch

Food coloring

❶ In medium-size pan dissolve cornstarch in boiling water. Add food coloring, and bring mixture to a boil again. Cool, and paint!

Salt Paint

1 cup flour

1 cup salt

1 cup water

1 teaspoon food coloring

❶ Combine all ingredients. Spoon into a pastry tube, and squeeze onto heavy paper.

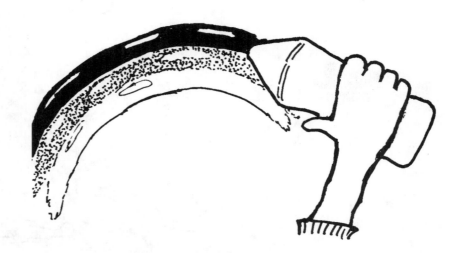

Index

Boldface numbers indicate recipe titles. Items in capital letters are brand names.

Popular Books by Starburst Publishers®

Allergy Cooking with Ease: The No Wheat, Milk, Eggs, Corn, Soy, Yeast, Sugar, Grain, and Gluten Cookbook

By Nicolette M. Dumke

A book designed to provide a wide variety of recipes to meet many different dietary and social needs, and whenever possible, save you time in food preparation. Includes recipes for foods that food allergy patients think they will never eat again, as well as time-saving tricks and an Allergen Avoidance index.

(trade paper)   ISBN 091498442X   **$14.95**

The Weekly Feeder: A Revolutionary Shopping, Cooking, and Meal-Planning System

By Cori Kirkpatrick

A revolutionary meal-planning system that makes preparing home-cooked dinners more convenient than ever. At the beginning of each week, simply choose one of the eight preplanned menus, tear out the corresponding grocery list, do your shopping, and whip up each fantastic meal in less than 45 minutes! The author's household management tips, equipment checklists, and nutrition information make this system a must for any busy family. Included with every recipe is a personal anecdote from the author emphasizing the importance of good food, a healthy family, and a well-balanced life.

(trade paper)   ISBN 1892016095   **$16.95**

Cheap Talk with the Frugal Friends

By Angie Zalewski and Deana Ricks

A collection of savvy tips and tricks for stretching the family dollar from celebrity thrifters, Angie Zalewski and Deana Ricks, known as the Frugal Friends by their radio and television audiences. This book features twenty-nine chapters on various topics including automotive, beauty care, cleaning products, dating, decorating, entertainment, medicine, pet care, sporting goods, and more. Includes special chapters on eliminating credit card debt, making extra money, and organizing the home. Finally, a practical way to save money without compromising convenience or lowering lifestyle standards!

(trade paper)   ISBN 1892016583   **$9.99**

The Bible—God's Word for the Biblically-Inept™

By Larry Richards

An excellent book to start learning the entire Bible. Get the basics or the in-depth information you are seeking with this user-friendly overview, including icons, illustrations, and study questions. From Creation to Christ to the Millennium, learning the Bible has never been easier. The *God's Word for the Biblically-Inept™* series also includes *Revelation, Genesis, John, Romans,* and more.

(trade paper)   ISBN 0914984551   **$16.95**

God Things Come in Small Packages: Celebrating the Little Things in Life

By Susan Duke, LeAnn Weiss, Caron Loveless, and Judith Carden

Enjoy touching reminders of God's simple yet generous gifts to brighten our days and gladden our hearts! Treasures like a sunset over a vast, sparkling ocean; a child's trust; or the crystalline dew on a spider's web come to life in this elegant compilation. Such occasions should be celebrated as if gift wrapped from God; they're his hallmarks! Personalized Scripture is artfully combined with compelling stories and reflections. (hard cover)   ISBN 1892016281   **$12.95**

Purchasing Information
www.starburstpublishers.com

Books are available from your favorite bookstore, either from current stock or special order. To assist bookstores in locating your selection, be sure to give title, author, and ISBN. If unable to purchase from a bookstore, you may order direct from STARBURST PUBLISHERS. When ordering please enclose full payment plus shipping and handling as follows:

Post Office (4th class)
$4.00 with a purchase of
   up to $20.00
$5.00 ($20.01–$50.00)
9% of purchase price for
   purchases of $50.01 and up

Canada
$5.00 (up to $35.00)
15% ($35.01 and up)

United Parcel Service (UPS)
$5.00 (up to $20.00)
$7.00 ($20.01–$50.00)
12% ($50.01 and up)

Overseas
$5.00 (up to $25.00)
20% ($25.01 and up)

Payment in U.S. funds only. Please allow two to four weeks minimum for delivery by USPS (longer for overseas and Canada). Allow two to seven working days for delivery by UPS.

Make checks payable to and mail to:

Starburst Publishers®
P.O. Box 4123
Lancaster, PA 17604

Credit card orders may be placed by calling 1-800-441-1456, Mon.–Fri., 8:30 A.M. to 5:30 P.M. Eastern Standard Time. Prices are subject to change without notice. Catalogs are available for a 9 x 12 self-addressed envelope with four first-class stamps.